Patch of Blue and 3 hearts canvas
in association with
Southwark Playhouse and Verse Unbound

CASSIE AND THE LIGHTS

BY ALEX HOWARTH

T0347579

Cassie and the Lights opened at Southwark Playhouse, London,
on 3 April 2024.

CASSIE AND THE LIGHTS

BY ALEX HOWARTH

Cassie	**Alex Brain**
Tin	**Helen Chong**
Kit	**Emily McGlynn**
Musicians	**Ellie and Imogen Mason**
Super Swing	**Martha Walker**

With the voices of

Alice	**Louisa Harland**
Mark	**Oli Higginson**
Jasmine	**Bethany Antonia**
Teacher	**Wendi Peters**
Lawyer	**John Thomson**
Social Worker	**Sam Rayner**
Dealer	**Joseph Stevens**

Writer, Director & Original Scenic Design	**Alex Howarth**
Co-Composers	**Ellie & Imogen Mason**
Lighting Designer	**Will Monks**
Video Designer	**Rachel Sampley**
Set Designer	**Ruth Badila**
Production Manager	**Erratic Imagination Technical Services**
Stage Manager	**Lauren Cross**
Graphic Design	**Casey Jay Andrews**
Producer	**Patch of Blue** and **3 hearts canvas** in association with **Southwark Playhouse** and **Verse Unbound**
Press	**Kate Morley PR**

Cassie and the Lights is based on a true story and interviews with care-experienced children and young people. It was first performed at VAULT Festival, London, from 31st January 2020. It was subsequently performed at Adelaide Fringe, Australia, from 14th February 2020 where it won Best Theatre Award. It ran at Underbelly, Edinburgh Fringe from 4th August 2022 where it was nominated for the Popcorn Award and the SIT-UP Award for social change, as well as being listed in the Best Theatre of the Edinburgh Fringe in *The Stage* by Lyn Gardner. It then closed the Brits Off Broadway season at 59E59 Theaters, Off Broadway, New York from 13th June 2023, before transferring to Southwark Playhouse, London, from 3rd April 2024.

Alex Howarth | Writer, Director, Original Scenic Design

Alex is an award-winning theatre director and writer based in London. He was named one of 'Ten Stage Sensations to Watch Out For in 2023' by *Guardian*. Coming from the North West and with a background of working in care, Alex is passionate about amplifying under-represented and northern voices.

His upcoming work includes *Lifeline* – an original Scottish folk musical about the antibiotic resistance crisis, which will open at Signature Theatre, Off Broadway, New York in August 2024, and features a chorus of real-life doctors and nurses.

Cassie and the Lights was based on a true story and interviews with children in the care system. Nominated for the Popcorn Award and the SIT-UP Award for social change, it ran at 59E59 Theaters, Off Broadway, New York in 2023. A former dramatherapist for the charity Sense, he has worked extensively with disabled artists, and recently co-created one-man show *Strictly Lawrie* with Lawrie Morris, star of *Growing Up Downs* (BBC).

His play about a girl with autism, *We Live By The Sea*, received Critic's Pick and Top Theatre of the Year in *The New York Times*, won the Best Theatre Award and the Critic's Choice Award at Adelaide Fringe, and the Graham F. Smith Peace Foundation Award for promoting human rights through theatre, and was nominated for the Fringe First and the Off-West-End Awards for Best Production and Best Ensemble.

He was the assistant director on *La Traviata* at the Royal Opera House, Covent Garden, and regularly directs at drama schools including Arts Educational Schools, Italia Conti, Central School of Speech and Drama, Mountview, and Chichester Conservatoire. He adapted and directed the world stage premiere of *What's Eating Gilbert Grape*, alongside the movie's writer and director, Academy Award nominee Peter Hedges. He is the Artistic Director of multi-award winning Patch of Blue, who create original theatre pieces with live music for festivals and touring.

He strives to create ensemble-led theatre that is playful, fresh and moving.

Alex Brain | Cassie

Alex Brain started off as a child actor starring in *Primeval* and BBC's *Enid*, where they played the twelve-year old Enid Blyton. Alex also played Nigella in *The Railway Children* at Waterloo for York Theatre Royal.

As an adult actor they have worked extensively with Alex Howarth in productions such as *Back to Blackbrick*, *The Illness Should Attend*, *When We Ran*, *The Tortoise and the Hare* and the highly acclaimed *We Live By The Sea*, which played in London, Edinburgh, New York, and Adelaide. They first appeared in *Cassie And The Lights* at VAULT Festival, then at Adelaide Fringe, the Edinburgh Festival and New York. Most recently they toured across Australia and New Zealand with Wright&Grainger's *The Gods The Gods The Gods*.

Helen Chong | Tin

Helen first trained at Musical Theatre Studio (2018 – 2022) and The Mark Jermin Stage School (2020 – 2023). She then moved on to study at Guildford School of Acting, on their foundation musical theatre course (2022 – 2023).

Helen recently performed off-Broadway, where she was the Super Swing in *Cassie And The Lights* (59E59 Theaters).

Her other credits on stage include Eloper in *Alice In Wonderlust* (Lawrence Batley Theatre), Keeley in *Orca* (Laurels Whitley Bay), Swing/1st cover Belle/Dance Captain in *Beauty and the Beast* (Venue No1), A in *Four Models in Bright Hats Think About the Future* (Live Theatre Newcastle), Annie in *Jack and the Beanstalk* (Applecart Arts) Ensemble/Onstage Swing in *Cinderella* (Gala Theatre) and *Haddaway & Write* (Gala Theatre and The Exchange).

On screen, she has played Nina in *The Dumping Ground* (CBBC), Jenny in *Casualty* (BBC) and Amy in *The Hermit* (YouTube). Helen has also been involved in various music videos and educational projects.

Credits whilst training: Performer/Dance Captain in *What Comes Next?* (Guildford School of Acting).

Emily McGlynn | Kit

Emily is a Liverpool-based performer. She graduated in 2018 from Liverpool Theatre School.

Credits include *The Fall* (Old Red Lion Theatre), *Long Joan Silver*

(Hope St Theatre), *Oh! You Pretty Things* (Southwark Playhouse), *Aladdin* (Palace Theatre), *Jose* (Liverpool Fringe), *Piramania! The Swashbuckling Pirate Musical* (Upstairs at the Gatehouse and Edinburgh Fringe), *Cassie and the Lights* (VAULT Festival, Adelaide Fringe Festival, Edinburgh Fringe and 59E59 Theaters, New York).

Credits whilst training: Moon in *Blood Wedding*, and Gaoler's Daughter in *The Wind in the Willows*.

Imogen Mason & Ellie Mason | Musicians & Composers

Imogen and Ellie Mason are musicians, producers, and composers from Kent, UK. They are two members of the band Voka Gentle. They have a long-standing working relationship with Patch of Blue, and have scored many plays for them including *We Live By The Sea* (59E59 Theaters, Arts Theatre West End, and touring), *Back to Blackbrick* (Arts Theatre West End and touring), and *The Tortoise and the Hare* (touring).

Martha Walker | Swing

Cassie and the Lights is Martha's professional stage debut. Martha graduated in 2023 from Italia Conti and her credits whilst training include Tobias in *Sweeney Todd*, and *Big Fish*.

Louisa Harland | Alice

Before commencing her training at Mountview, Louisa appeared as a series regular in *Love/Hate* for RTE alongside Aidan Gillen and

Robert Sheehan. Further screen credits include Channel 5's *The Deceived*, Discovery's mini-series *Harley and the Davidsons*, Woody Harrelson's feature film *Lost in London* and Jack Rooke's award winning comedy *Big Boys*. In 2022, the third and final season of *Derry Girls* aired to wide-spread critical acclaim.

On stage Louisa starred in the one woman show *Cotton Fingers* with National Theatre Wales and performed in a sell-out run at the Royal Court of *Glass. Kill. Bluebeard. Imp*; a collection of new plays by Caryl Churchill. Most recently she starred as Agnes in *Dancing At Lughnasa* at the National Theatre, directed by Josie Rourke, and in David Ireland's play *Ulster American* opposite Woody Harrelson and Andy Serkis.

Louisa played a leading role alongside Jack Rowan in the comedy/horror feature film *Boys From County Hell*, and she has recently wrapped *Joy* directed by Ben Taylor, where she features alongside Bill Nighy and James Norton.

Louisa will be playing the title role in Sally Wainwright's highly-anticipated new Disney+ series, *Renegade Nell* and can next be seen in *Long Day's Journey Into Night* in the West End opposite Brian Cox.

Oli Higginson | Mark

Oli recently starred in the new series of *Julia* for HBO opposite Sarah Lancashire, Stockard Channing and Isabella Rossellini. He can be seen alongside Adrian Scarborough in the latest season of *The Chelsea Detective* and will soon be appearing in season three of hit Netflix series *Bridgerton*, reprising his role from seasons one and two. Other television credits include Michael Winterbottom's Sky Atlantic show *This England*, Emily Mortimer's *The Pursuit Of Love* opposite Lily James for BBC and *Cursed* for Netflix.

Onstage, Oli has just played Cassio in the acclaimed production of Shakespeare's *Othello* in the Sam Wanamaker Playhouse at The Globe, directed by Ola Ince. He received a Stage Debut Award nomination for his performance as Jamie in the West End production of two-hander musical *The Last Five Years*, which transferred from Southwark Playhouse and was hailed by WhatsOnStage as the 'definitive production'. Other stage work includes *The Haystack* directed by Roxana Silbert at Hampstead Theatre, *A Christmas Carol* directed by Matthew Warchus at The Old Vic, the London Premieres of *Lava* (Soho Theatre) and *Smoke* (Southwark Playhouse), *Napoleon Blown Apart* (Arcola Theatre), and *Maggie & Ted* (West End).

Film includes *Treadmill*, and *Pipe Dream* written and directed by Misha Seresin.

Radio includes *Doctor Who* and *If We are Moses*.

Rehearsed readings and workshops include *Girl, Woman, Other* (National Theatre Studio), *The Cracks* (Criterion Theatre), *Tandle Hill* (National Theatre Studio), *Perkin Warbeck* (Theatre Royal

Stratford East), *Dear Octopus* (National Theatre Studio), and *The Witches* directed by Lyndsey Turner (National Theatre Studio).

Oli is also an emerging writer, currently developing his debut play alongside the Orange Tree Theatre as part of the Orange Tree's Writers Collective, whose alumni include Chris Bush, Sonali Bhattacharyya, Jade Anouka, and Joe White.

Oli trained as an actor at the Guildhall School of Music and Drama, graduating in 2019.

Bethany Antonia | Jasmine

Bethany can be seen in the new series of *House Of The Dragon* (HBO) as Baela Targaryen. Other television includes *Nolly* (ITV/ Quay Street) opposite Helena Bonham Carter, *Stay Close* (Red Production Company/Netflix), *Get Even* (BBC/Netflix), *Stath Lets Flats* (Roughcut / C4) and *Doctors* (BBC).

Film includes *Indignitas* (short) (Transition Film Company), *There's Always Hope* (Bad Penny Productions), *Pin Cushion* (BFI), and *The Tempest* (short) (Shakespeare Birthplace Trust).

Voiceover includes *The Velveteen Rabbit* (Magic Light Productions), *Doctor Who: Far From Home* (Big Finish), and *Dark Season: Legacy Rising* (Big Finish).

Theatre includes *Lava* (Soho Theatre), *Look Up* (Birmingham Think Tank), and *Peter Pan: The Never Ending Story World Arena Tour* (Birmingham National Indoor Arena).

Wendi Peters | Teacher

Wendi was recently seen in BBC1's *Doctors* as series regular Nina Bulsar, as well as playing Lynda Babbage in *Midsomer Murders* (ITV) and headlining the National Tour of *The Legend of Sleepy Hollow*.

Wendi is best known for her portrayal of the iconic Cilla Battersby-Brown in *Coronation Street*, and as series regular Cook Jenkins in *Hetty Feather* for CBBC.

Alongside her screen work Wendi is in much demand as a stage actress with recent credits including; Diane in the European Premiere of *You Are Here* (Southwark Playhouse), Madame Latour in the National Tour of John Cleese's *Bang Bang*, Mrs Baskin in the West End premiere of *Big The Musical* at the Dominion Theatre, *Call Me Vicky* (Pleasance Theatre), *Quartet* (National Tour), *State Fair* (Cadogan Hall), *Hatched 'n' Dispatched* (Park Theatre, London), *Oh What A Lovely War* (National Tour), *White Christmas* (Lowry, Manchester, Edinburgh Festival Theatre & Dominion Theatre, West End), *The Mystery Of Edwin Drood* at the Arts Theatre, West End and *Rutherford & Son* for Northern Broadsides on National Tour.

John Thompson | Lawyer

An award-winning actor, writer, comedian and presenter, John has been at the forefront of British television, film and theatre for over three decades.

John began his career voicing the puppets on the satirical *Spitting Image*. After winning the Perrier award in 1992 with Steve Coogan, John went on to work and write with Steve in the popular *Paul Calf Video Diaries* (BAFTA Winner) and has starred in many TV productions including *Men Behaving Badly*, *Coronation Street*, *Waterloo Road* and *New Street Law* (RTS nominated for best actor) and *The Fast Show* for BBC2. However, John is probably best remembered for his role as Pete Gifford in the multi-award-winning *Cold Feet* for ITV.

John's numerous film credits include *Wallace And Gromit: Curse Of The Were-Rabbit*, *24 Hour Party People* and *Grimsby*. John is a renowned vocal artist and has voiced a range of shows and films, including *Dog Loves Books* (CBBC), *Police Interceptors* as well as *Bargain Loving Brits In The Sun* and *Bargain Loving Brits By The Sea*.

He has also been a staple of light entertainment appearing in *Zone Of Champions*, *The Keith Lemon Sketch Show*, *The Keith And Paddy Film Show*, *Masterchef* and *The Masked Singer*.

John occasionally still dabbles in the dark art of stand-up comedy, selling out venues across the country. He is also a professional drummer and in his free time can be found playing his Gretsch and Roland V drums, as seen on *Gareth Malone's All Star Music Quiz*.

In October 2013, John received a 'Legend of Industry' award from the Variety Club of Great Britain for his contributions to Comedy, Film, Television and Theatre.

Will Monks | Lighting Designer

Will Monks is a lighting and video designer for theatre and live events. A Bristol Old Vic Theatre School graduate, his practice is centred around technology in aid of art and using access tools as creative techniques. Driven by collaboration and variety he is always exploring new ways in which the world can be seen.

Recognition includes *Offie Awards: OnComm For Young People 12+* Winner for *I Cinna (The Poet)*, (Unicorn Theatre*)*, Best Lighting Designer twice nominee for *Foxes* (Seven Dials Playhouse) and *The Dark Room* (Theatre503), Best Video Designer twice nominee for *Foxes (*Seven Dials Playhouse) and *Ali & Dahlia* (Pleasance London), UK Theatre Awards: Best Show for Children & Young People nominee for *Petula* (National Theatre Wales & Theatr Genedlaethol Cymru), Fringe First Award and Amnesty International Freedom of Expression Award winner for *Trojan Horse* (Summerhall).

During the pandemic Will created and consulted on streamed and audience-at-home productions. Work includes *Open Mic* (English Touring Theatre), *I Cinna (The Poet)* (Unicorn Theatre), a digital production of Tim Crouch's *My Arm* (Shedinburgh and Santiago a Mil festivals), *Sunnymead Court* (Defibrillator) which was nominated for four Offies including Best Production; and *The Great Big*

Story Mix Up (Roustabout Theatre); an improvised online family show in which the audience's drawings are used in the video design.

Will also teaches lighting and video design, running workshops and tutoring students. He is currently an Associate Lecturer at Wimbledon College of Art (part of University of the Arts London).

Rachel Sampley | Video Designer

Rachel is a London-based video and lighting designer. Theatre includes *Barriers* (National Theatre), *Follow the Signs* (Soho Theatre), *Opal Fruits* (Bristol Old Vic and Pleasance Edinburgh), *Cassie and the Lights* (VAULT Festival, Adelaide Fringe, Underbelly and 59E59 Theaters) and *Perfect Show for Rachel* (Barbican).

Ruth Badila | Set Designer

Ruth Badila trained at University of the Arts, Wimbledon, graduating in 2020. She then worked as an associate assistant designer at the Kiln Theatre. Ruth has recently completed a year's residency as Assistant Designer at the National Theatre. She is a previous recipient of the Linbury Prize 2021.

Lauren Cross | Stage Manager

Lauren grew up an active and engaged member in her local theatre scene as both performer and technician. She studied at the University of Cumbria specialising in performing arts and technical theatre.

After graduating she worked in a diverse range of roles, including stage management, stage crew and sound technician. Her most recent projects include working with the Rhiannon Faith Dance Company on their Olivier Award-nominated *Lay Down Your Burdens* (Barbican) as well as *Drowntown* (UK and China tour). She has developed her skills by working for the last two years as a venue technician at the Edinburgh Fringe for Underbelly where she first saw *Cassie and the Lights*. Lauren is grateful to be working with Patch of Blue and excited for people to continue to experience this show and the heartfelt story that it tells.

Erratic Imagination Technical Services | Production Manager

Erratic Imagination Technical Services was formed in 2023 with the dual goals of providing sustainable world class technical support to the live events industry and helping new technicians, particularly those in rural areas enter the business.

Helmed by Darren Minto, with over two decades experience in the industry, and staffed by a mix of new and experienced technicians, EITS provides technical services with sustainability and innovation at their core. EITS also provides a full Production Management service specialising in non-traditional venues and since formation have worked with several touring opera and ballet companies to take shows into rural communities and settings.

Casey Jay Andrews | Graphic Design

Casey Jay Andrews is a multi-award winning writer, designer and theatre-maker based in the South East of England (though her heart is planted firmly in Edinburgh's Old Town).

Casey is Senior Designer at *Punchdrunk Enrichment* and previously worked as Assistant Head of Design on Punchdrunk International's *The Burnt City*.

As a writer, Casey won a Fringe First Award for her play *The Archive of Educated Hearts* at the 2018 Edinburgh Festival Fringe. It had its North American debut in December 2019 at The Soho Playhouse New York, the same theatre where Phoebe Waller-Bridge's *Fleabag* and Hannah Gadsby's *Nanette* debuted in NYC.

Other plays include *A Place That Belongs To Monsters*, *The Wild Unfeeling World* and *Oh My Heart, Oh My Home*.

As a Designer, Casey has an eclectic design background ranging from large scale immersive theatre design, to mural painting and carved wooden puppets. Casey has a particular interest in intimate narrative led installations; these have provided a home for many of her writing and storytelling projects. She has previously designed for Francesca Moody Productions, Imogen Heap, BT Sport, Shotgun Carousel, Rabble Theatre and *The Immersive Great Gatsby* in London, New York and Seoul.

Patch of Blue create fresh, exciting and touching theatre with live music. They are currently producing Alex Howarth's *Cassie and the Lights* – an award-winning play with music they have brought to London, Australia, Edinburgh and New York.

They are the recipient of the prestigious Graham F. Smith Peace Foundation Award for promoting social change through theatre, Critic's Pick and Best Theatre of the Year in the *New York Times*, Best Theatre of Edinburgh Fringe in *The Stage* and two Best Theatre awards at Adelaide Fringe.

3HC
3 hearts canvas

3 hearts canvas is a London-based production house, led by artistic directors Meaghan Martin and Oli Higginson. They work to excavate the '3 hearts' of theatre, film, and music to develop provocative, challenging, and socially-conscious entertainment with a strong community backbone.

Working in both the commercial and subsidised sectors, their work has been regularly supported and championed by Arts Council England and The Carne Trust, and has been seen at theatres including Yard Theatre, Southwark Playhouse, Bush Theatre, Arcola Theatre, and Park Theatre.

Recent work includes the London Premiere of *SMOKE* (Southwark Playhouse, 2023; ★★★★ WhatsOnStage; ★★★★★ The Arts Desk) and the World Premiere of *SPIN* (Edinburgh Fringe 2023, and Arcola Theatre 2024; ★★★★ The Scotsman; ★★★★★ Theatre Weekly) which received an Off-Fest and Off-West End Nomination as well as being named Theatre Weekly's Best Solo Performance at the Edinburgh Festival Fringe 2023.

3 hearts canvas is passionate about championing teams and projects which reflect the diverse fabric of the communities that make the UK thrive, inspired by Arts Council England's Creative Case for Diversity initiative. They use sustainable practices wherever possible with a minimal ecological footprint, in partnership with the Green Theatre plan.

CASSIE AND THE LIGHTS

Alex Howarth

Characters

CASSIE, *seventeen years old*
TIN, *ten years old*
KIT, *seven years old*

MUSICIAN

Setting

Yorkshire

Notes for Performance

Other characters are recorded voices.

A slash (/) indicates an interruption.

A lack of punctuation at the end of a line indicates an unfinished thought.

In the original production, animation of the sisters was projected to represent Cassie's animation project. If you choose not to create this, the line referencing it may be cut.

This text went to press before the end of rehearsals and so may differ slightly from the play as performed.

The sisters – CASSIE, TIN and KIT – greet the audience.
CASSIE finds someone to read the court hearing, TIN finds
someone who she'll talk to in the 'The Audience' section, and
KIT offers around Party Rings. The MUSICIAN plays fun
space related songs.

TIN (*to the lighting operator*). Are we ready _____? Okay.
(*Into a mic, to the audience. Clears her throat.*) Hello
everyone, my name is Tin and welcome to my TED Talk, or,
Tin Talk, because my name is Tin and I'll be talking. And
today, what I'll be talking about is… trinary star systems.

KIT. Tri means three.

TIN. It does. (*Comes off the mic and turns to* CASSIE.) Cassie –
did we put new batteries in the fairy lights?

CASSIE. Duracell…

KIT. Love the bunny

TIN. And Kit did you practise?

KIT. Yeah, Elephant and Mr Potato Head said I did dead well.

TIN. Okay sorted. (*Turns back to the audience and talks into the*
mic again.) Then the Tin Talk will begin.

Scene One – Trinary Star Systems

Beautiful electronic space music. As TIN speaks, CASSIE
and KIT illustrate what she's saying using homemade props.
Although they have made it themselves, it should be beautiful
and spectacular, as if we are taking a voyage inside their heads.

TIN. A trinary star system is three stars that travel together in the sky when we look at them through our telescopes. Each one of the three stars orbits, which basically means flies, around the centre of the mass of the system (or the middle bit), pulled together by gravity, usually in what is called a 'hierarchical arrangement', which basically means that two of the stars are super-close, and one is a little bit further away – because if it wasn't a little bit further away the system would get unstable and one of the stars would be thrown out of the system forever and ever, amen. If you don't have the little-bit-further-away star, the system becomes what is called a 'trapezia' which does 'chaotic behaviour', which is very complicated maths that we haven't done at school yet but basically means they fight and you never know what they're going to do or what's going to happen to them, which is an especially bad and scary thing. But if there is this 'hierarchical arrangement', the trinary star system is stable and full of happy, and the stars move together through the universe, knowing that they are safe and can shine bright on the journey, and that they'll never, ever, be... alone. That is the end of the Tin Talk.

The sisters bow, CASSIE *and* KIT *giving* TIN *a special bow – her face glows with the applause and praise.*

Scene Two – Introductions

TIN. Now that the science-y bit is done

CASSIE. Thank you for listening

KIT. We should say hello proper.

ALL. Hello!

TIN. We are Tin and Kit and Cassie and when this all started we were ten and seven and sixteen

KIT. She's dead old

TIN. ...and when we were born and little we lived in a house with our mum

KIT. Playing out and oven chips

TIN. And cos me and Kit coming out of her were surprises she didn't know what to call us

CASSIE. So she named them after things she liked. And she were proper into Tina Turner...

TIN. So she called me Tina, but I wanted my own name so I made it shorter to Tin.

CASSIE. And then she got really into them videos of kittens on her phone – being cute and falling off of things

KIT. So she called me Kitten... but I made it shorter to Kit too like Tin did, cos kittens are well boring I'd rather have a pterodactyl.

TIN. But right now we live with Mark and Alice who are very kind and live in a big and tall house

KIT. Smells like soap

TIN. And our friends at school said is it like Tracy Beaker /

KIT. / and I said who's Tracy Beaker is she in Year 6 and they said don't you have a TV and I said we did until Mum sold it and they said okay and then we played British Bulldog

CASSIE. There's a TV at Mark and Alice's

TIN. Fifty-five inches

CASSIE. And when the girls have gone to bed and I've finished my homework I can watch the stuff my mates do – and I can talk about it with them in t'lunch queue instead of just... nodding along.

TIN. And they've got loadsa books too, that they got for kids they've had stay before – dead-good stories about having journeys and flying and little houses on prairies

KIT. We like stories

TIN. And this is our one.

CASSIE. That we'll tell to you now – if you're stopping

TIN. It's an hour and a bit, and there'll be time afterwards for orange squash and thinking

KIT. _____ does the music

TIN. And there's the drawings Cassie's done of us on the video

KIT. It's well snazzy like

CASSIE. There's going backwards and forwards in time which can get a bit confusing – but we hope in a good way

TIN. And there are some bits that are a bit sad – but we hope in a good way...

KIT. And there are lots of bits that are a bit fun – but in a good way... like fun always is

TIN. And we're very... elated you came... so thank you.

ALL. Thank you very much!

KIT (*whispered to them*). Okay – three, two, one, then blast-off, ready? (*Out.*) three, two, one

ALL. BLAST-OFF!

Scene Three – School / Home / Social Services – January 2023

All talk out. Horrible overwhelming sound builds underneath.

The shared words should land at the same time.

TEACHER. Hi.
Come in and
take a seat.

I've asked Miss
Johns to sit in
too.

You know why
I've called you
in Cassie.

TIN. Cassie where's my PE shorts?
I put them in t'laundry basket
but they aren't on t'drying rack
now

TEACHER. Now
I've already
extended your
animation project
deadline once

KIT. Once you've done that can we
play dinosaurs please?

There is gonna be a CALAMITY
if we don't!

…if you don't get
it to me this week
I'm going to have
to fail you on the
module.

I need you to
talk to me…

KIT. Talk to meeee! It's dead
urgent right cos there's
an emergency in the
velociraptor cave and Dora
the Explorer can't get out…

TEACHER. Please

Pleeeease…

don't ignore me.

LETTER. Don't ignore not a circular,
your benefits have lapsed as you
have not been actively seeking
work

Your work is
the strongest in
the class – you
have SO MUCH

potential are
you just going
to throw that
away
Cassie?

KIT. Cassie I'm still hungry, are you
sure you don't have something in
the back of the cupboard, like,
right at the back like? We'll
have to go to Asda if you
don't

LETTER. if you
don't make
payment now
you will receive
a court summons.
This is the
final time we
will ask

TIN. I asked Mrs Chang if we could
borrow a blanket from school cos the
house is dead cold and now she wants
to speak to Mum...

DEALER. Tell
your mum she
owes me money

What'll I tell her?

TEACHER. Cassie
I...

CASSIE. Will
you get off
my back?

KIT. My back's got these funny red spots
on

TEACHER.
Cassie...

Cassie

CASSIE. No y'know what, right, how the hell am I supposed
to do this

TEACHER.
Cassie...

TIN. Cassie my school tights are ripped

CASSIE. You FUCKING TELL ME

HOW   how'll we get new ones, Pavithra
                              Gupta called me a dirty povvo
KIT. They're   it were
    horrible itchy   horrible

TEACHER.
    Cassandra   LETTER. Mrs
    Braithwaite   Braithwaite

                                                    CASSIE. Y'know
                                                        what
                                                        what's the
LETTER. Your   fucking point
    court hearing
    has been set
    for nineteenth
    December   CASSIE.…you're
                                                        not listening
                              TIN. Cassie, Kit's
                                  sweaty but she's
                                  shivering

KIT. I'm scared   I'm scared
    Cassie I had
    a dream that
    Mum were dead

                                                    CASSIE. Fuck this

KIT. Cassie is she
    dead?

TEACHER. Stop behaving like a child

CASSIE. I am not a fucking child!!

Scene Four – Home / Social Services – January 2023

There is a loud knock. The scene is now played realistically. They all look at the door.

TIN. Cassie… Cassie, who's that at door?

KIT. It's Mum! Cassie it's Mum (*Runs towards the door.*)

CASSIE. No Kit wait just… I'm sure it's her just… let me look first, eh?

She goes to the window in the door and opens the curtain slightly.

(*Quietly.*) Fuck.

KIT. She must be soaking – has she got her umbrella?

CASSIE. Girls listen /

KIT. / Cos she an't got her mac, it's hanging on t'back o' kitchen door

CASSIE. Kit it's not her…

TIN. What?

CASSIE. Did you tell someone? Cos I said not to /

KIT. / Well who is it then?

CASSIE. Did you tell someone at school?

TIN. No… /

KIT. / Let me look… (*Goes to the window in the door.*)

CASSIE. / Or someone from up the road… /

TIN *looks away.*

KIT. / Who are they?

CASSIE. Tin…

TIN. Kit told Mrs Phillips from the flats…

KIT. They look nice…

TIN....we saw her when you sent us to pick up the loo roll in Asda while you got the apples

Knock again.

KIT. Do you think they'll be able to fix the electricity?

CASSIE (*to herself*). But she's gonna come back. She's gonna come back, they can't...

Knock again.

KIT. Shall I let them in then, Cassie?

No response.

Cassie?

CASSIE. I'll do it. Kit give your sister a hug. And don't let go until I'm back.

Music and recordings of social workers' voices asking the following, the voices build, repeat and overlap.

The sisters listen.

VOICES. Do you mind if there's a man there?

What about if there's a dog?

What school was it you went to?

Do you have a toy you want to bring?

What are your hobbies?

What football team do you support?

Music out. They are in the Social Services' office. KIT *is listening at the office door.*

KIT. Can't believe he took us in a Ford Mondeo... Chloe Lee from school'll be dead impressed.

TIN. What are they doing in there, Kit?

KIT. Hey Cassie he said when he were done he'd get me one of them Cokes with vanilla in – dead exotic...

TIN. You can't have Coke; it's almost ten o'clock!

KIT (*looking round the room*). Them pictures are dead nice – rainbows and flowers and happy things like in films... Oh, he's coming...

She runs back to CASSIE *and* TIN.

Hiya.

They turn to address the audience.

TIN. And they told us they'd found someone.

KIT. So we got another go in the Ford Mondeo. It were raining super-hard all the way there – Cassie called it pathetic fallacy – I just called it wet.

CASSIE. Tin kept asking what would happen when Mum came back. But West Yorkshire County Council were our mum now. And Mark and Alice's house were our new home.

Transition – Lawyer (Audio)

The sisters hear the following recording. Not wanting to listen to it, they busy themselves with setting up the next scene.

CASSIE. Dan... if they judge against me and Mark and Alice adopt them – could they cut our contact?

LAWYER. Yes, but I'm sure from what you've told me...

CASSIE. But they could?

Scene Five – Bowling – February 2023

Bowling alley sounds. The sisters sit on the floor and watch people bowl.

KIT. He's got my bowling ball.

TIN. That bloke?

KIT. That bloke. If you look dead hard you can see 'Kit' scratched on t'bottom. Who's got yours, Tin?

TIN. Mine's super-faded now – I need to bring my compass again next Bowling Wednesday. How many games can we have Cassie?

KIT. And did Alice give you money for slushies after? I want blue flavour, please.

CASSIE. We can have one game – or Kit'll be too tired for school in t'morning – yes she gave me slushie money and no you cannot have blue she'll kill me! Have red – least it looks like it's got some vitamins in.

Pause. They watch the bowling.

Eh I got my animation project handed in… Miss Jacobson really liked it… you know the one I filmed you both for on t'school camera. She said fingers crossed they might put it on t'school YouTube channel.

KIT. Fingers crossed and toes crossed! They're inside my shoes so you can't tell

TIN. Have you got the letter for Mum?

CASSIE. It's in my backpack. I'll put it in the secret spot just before we go.

TIN. And you'll check she took last week's? Like she took the week before's?

CASSIE. I'll check. I told her all about you going up a set in maths.

KIT. And me finishing my Build A Dinosaur from t'Oxfam shop

CASSIE (*proud*). I told her all about that too.

They watch the bowling again.

TIN. Do you think she's here somewhere? Hiding like. Cos this is the last place we saw her – and now we come here every week

KIT.…Bowling Wednesday.

CASSIE. What? Tin why would she be hiding?

TIN. Like to check on us. That we're okay like

KIT. ...and that we're remembering to like wash our hands and breathe and love each other

TIN. ...and then once she'd seen that we were, she'd do a smile, then take your letter and go back to... well... whatever it is that she's doing. I bet that's what she does.

CASSIE. Maybe... Eh, how were school? Did you hold Tin's hand when you crossed t'road this time?

KIT. Yeah I did thanks and it were okay thanks Billy Jackson were dead loud at break and tried to embarrass me but I would not be embarrassed

CASSIE. Jesus Christ... What did he say and what did you say?

KIT. He just said stupid stuff like, cos he knows Mum went on holidays and about Mark and Alice, and he said dead loud so everyone on t'climbing frame could hear, 'What'd you have for your tea last night, were it baked beans out the tin?' and I said 'No Billy we had cous cous.' And none of 'em knew what cous cous were... except Chloe Lee, cos she knows about all foods. She's right trendy. Her dog's on Instagram.

CASSIE. How'd he know about Mark and Alice and all that? It's only been three weeks.

TIN. I told Jake Hawkins – as a secret, like – and he told Shivani Jeyapragesh as a secret like and she told Mercedes Kennedy as a secret like 'cept Mercedes Kennedy dun't know what a secret is, and the whole playground knew by afternoon break.

CASSIE. Well it sounds like you smashed it – proper showed Billy Jackson what for.

TIN. She were sad for a minute, weren't y'...

KIT. Yeah, but then I just shook it off, like Taylor Swift does.

They shake it off, like Taylor Swift does. A moment of quiet again. CASSIE *looks at them as they watch the bowling.*

CASSIE. Hey, listen to me for a minute, yeah… we have to not get used to this right… actually bowling not just watching… cous cous and a slushie each and Netflix and stuff. Cos we don't know how long Mark and Alice'll have us and if we'll have to pack up again and go… somewhere. You know that yeah?

TIN. It's alright, we won't have time to get used to owt

CASSIE. Good.

KIT. Yeah, cos Mum'll be back soon! We'll have to take some cous cous with us when we go.

CASSIE (*beat*). Yeah. Yeah course. (*She looks up and sees people leaving.*) Oh, lane's free. Ready?

ALL. Three, two, one, blast-off!

They stand up ready to bowl. TIN *looks up at the neon lights above them.*

TIN. They're so beautiful – aren't they Cassie?

CASSIE (*smiling and looking back*). What are?

TIN. The lights!

Music.

Pink, and blue and orange neon

KIT. Colour all over us – it's like having a colour bath! And Mum used to sit and hold our hands in t'colour and we'd listen to the people doing the bowling and feel t'colour go into us… till we were bright again.

TIN. One day when we're here in the colour she'll come back. We'll see her walking to us in the pink and blue and orange and she'll hold our hands in t'colour and we'll go home together under all the golden street lights to our own house… for forever and ever amen. Won't we Cassie?

Music out.

Won't we?

Transition – Letter

Music. The MUSICIAN *puts their bowling-attendant cap on.*
CASSIE *hands them a letter from her bag, and while they read*
it CASSIE *plays with Mr Potatohead,* TIN *reads a space book*
and KIT *colours in.*

MUSICIAN. Hi Mum – it's Thursday again… Jasmine wanted
me to go round to hers tonight for movies but I said I'd pick
the girls up from school and make their tea cos Mark's still
at work, and Alice's got Pilates again. (*Beat.*) Apart from
that though being here's been a bit of a break for me. I've got
this big fancy bedroom just mine… they've even put a desk
in for me to do my homework on. Tuesday breakfast I said
I'd been wanting to see them Pixar short films and when I
got home they'd downloaded Disney Plus so I could watch
'em… the girls can finally watch *Frozen*! Oh, and Mark
keeps leaving uni brochures on my bed… As if I'm gonna…
So I know I should be nice to them, you'd probably think
they were toffs… and I'm trying but… (*Beat.*) It's not right
Mum. Being here. And I know it were so hard before; when I
counted the dole money wrong and all we had to eat for three
days were biscuits, or when I spent the electric money on
Christmas presents and it were freezing. But Mark and Alice
are not our family. I don't know what to do Mum… Where
are you? And when are you coming back? Anyway… I'd
better stop now – I want to make sure I'm there at the gate
when they're finished. Their smiles when they see me are…
little bits of magic. I'll write again next week – but… please
come back before then so I don't have to. Your daughter –
Cassie.

The MUSICIAN *looks at the letter, worried and confused,*
and checks the back for an address. They put it away and
take the cap off.

Scene Six – Meeting Mark and Alice – January 2023 (Audio)

The sisters play their home-made Jenga while a recording of the following plays:

MARK. Hello girls.

ALICE. It's lovely to meet you.

KIT. Is this really your house?

MARK. Er... yeah

KIT. It's dead lucky you only livin' on Castle Street y'know – the man from t'Social said they coulda sent us past Skipton

MARK. We just want you to know that we're going to do everything we can to make you feel at home when you're staying with us – we're going to Waitrose in the morning, and we can get anything you want, and...

KIT. What's Waitrose?

ALICE. Sorry?

CASSIE. It's like Asda but with fancy stuff /

KIT. / Love Asda

ALICE. Well...

CASSIE. / like chorizo and smashed avocado

KIT. Why would you smash an avocado? /

MARK. As I say... anything you want. No chorizo, I promise.

TIN. How long are we going to be at your house for? Like, till our mum comes back or...

CASSIE. / It's just for a few days Tin, till we get ourselves sorted

KIT. And Mum'll be back soon right – she's just... gone on holidays...

TIN. / So it won't be for very long...

KIT. Do you have a washing machine here cos I've only got one pair of clean pants left and Cassie says I can't just keep turning them inside out

TIN. How many days do YOU think we'll be here Cassie? /

ALICE. / We don't know how long it'll be... love... Let's just – take it one day at a time eh?

The girls stand and talk out. Music.

KIT. 'Take it one day at a time' is just what grown ups say when they want you to stop asking hard questions. Questions that make their brains sore

TIN. But hard questions are the best – like what is the universe made of?

KIT. Like if all the kind people got together and had a big think, could they make all the nasty people stop?

Music out.

CASSIE. Like what if our mum never comes back?

Lights change. We hear Jasmine's voice.

Scene Seven – Jasmine's House – March 2023

JASMINE. So basically she's just being a knob...

CASSIE. Jaz! Shut up, man

JASMINE. So you're my bestie now, sound good?

CASSIE (*flattered*). Yeah... sounds good.

JASMINE. I've got you the whole night right? You haven't got to go play mum? /

CASSIE. / No... Alice's putting the girls to bed, so...

Beat. Jasmine sees that CASSIE has mixed feelings about this.

JASMINE (*kindly*). Has she fucked off for good this time d'you think? Your mum.

CASSIE. No... no she'll turn up, she... she always does. Then we can get back to it just being the four of us, and /

JASMINE. / You're better off, Cass! Think about it – no more arsehole boyfriends smashing the living room up at three in the morning...

CASSIE. Jaz... /

JASMINE. / people after money banging the door down, scaring your sisters

CASSIE. Mate, please... /

JASMINE. / No y'know what I'm not having this again – she's a wreckhead Cass – making you stay in the bloody hospital room with her and watch while she had your sister, for fuck's sake... and you were what, ten?

CASSIE. Yeah.

JASMINE. I'm just sayin'...

She sees CASSIE *can't take any more and softens.*

Look wherever she is I bet she's happy... And if these two poshos babysitting means I get nights in with my bestie, how can that be a bad thing eh?

CASSIE. Yeah. Yeah course.

JASMINE. Good. Anyway, a thousand views wooohooo

CASSIE. What?

JASMINE. On our project!

CASSIE. Oh... yeah! That's pretty good that in't it... a thousand people.

JASMINE. Eh, that'll impress 'em when we get into that media production summer school thing we applied for

CASSIE. Yeah... yeah it will

JASMINE. I got summat to celebrate open t'drawer

CASSIE *takes a bottle of wine out.*

Aldi's finest...

CASSIE *holds it up so we see it's half empty.*

I er... may have started celebrating before you came

CASSIE. Oh... ta... (*Puts it aside.*)

JASMINE. I'm dead proud of you, you know...

CASSIE. Shut up man...

JASMINE. I will not shut up Cassandra Braithwaite – when you're head of Pixar, and I'm the next Quentin Tarantino, right

CASSIE. Well you are a visionary

JASMINE. I flipping am right anyway, when all that's happened we... will rule the world Cassandra Braithwaite. Them bright lights are waiting for us...

Music.

You and me...

CASSIE. Do you... do you really think we could, Jaz? Not the 'ruling the world' thing, but the film thing and... the Pixar thing... do you think we really could?

Ominous sound. Lights change slowly over the following recording.

This breaks CASSIE *out of her hope.*

Transition – Lawyer (Audio)

LAWYER. Just so we're clear – you're asking the court to put Tina and Kitten in your care. You can apply for a special guardianship order when you're eighteen, but until then we're proposing a child arrangement order, bolstered by a supervision order in favour of the local authority.

Lights change. TIN *and* KIT *are there.* CASSIE *is forced to shake off her fear.*

Scene Eight – Differences

CASSIE. Right, we're gonna do this bit now

TIN. Yus!! Can I go first?

CASSIE. You absolutely can

KIT. Can I go last?

CASSIE. You absolutely can

Improvised conversation before the sisters create a piece of music using loop pedals, which then underscores the following scene. TIN *and* KIT *project drawings of the things they are talking about using an overhead projector.*

KIT. Chloe Lee, who I sit next to at lunch, asked me and Tin today what were different about living with Mark and Alice instead of being at home with Mum.

TIN. And I started and said all the books they have – by people like Charles Dickens and Stephenie Meyer

KIT. Then I said the jar I found that said Waitrose Essential Artichoke Hearts 'cept I didn't know what an artichoke heart were so I googled it, and I don't really think artichoke hearts are essential I think they're just a treat

TIN. Mum likes the music we do, but Mark likes Wagner and Tchaikovsky

KIT. And he thought Ariana Grande was summat you get in Starbucks

TIN. Butter on our Dairylea sandwiches

KIT. And carpet that feels like a dead-soft sheep under your toes when you take your slippers off

TIN. That our bedroom isn't really our bedroom cos it's only our bedroom for a bit

KIT. And that our bedroom dun't have Tin's glow-in-the-dark stars on the ceiling she got out o t'space magazine

TIN. Or Kit's poster of an extra-long-trunked elephant on t'wall

KIT. Janice

TIN. Cos it's only for a few more days that we're here, probably

KIT. ...and we don't want to waste Blu Tac

TIN. That a social worker comes round every week and asks daft questions and fills out loads of forms and puts them in a box

KIT. That when we came we only had Mr Potato Head and Elephant, and the Jenga we made out of ice-lolly sticks

TIN. But they gave us lots more things they already had like Lego and Stickle Bricks which is mega-kind

KIT. ...but they don't go in our games, so they just sit there; and if they come to life when we're not looking like in *Toy Story* they'll be dead sad

TIN. That it dun't smell like our house

KIT. That Mum isn't there... and even though Mark and Alice are very nice, when it's bedtime and the lights are turned off... I feel Mum not being there in my tummy

Music out.

BOTH. That even when all the lights are on it feels like it is dark.

Transition – Slushie (Audio)

Unsettling sound. The sisters are reminded of the night their mum left, as the following recording plays. TIN is able to shake it off and set up for the next scene, but KIT remains centre, lost in the memory.

TIN. Kit it's alright – there's just a long line at t'slushie counter… I bet there is! Maybe machine's broken again and she's just waiting for 'em to fix it. Cassie'll go check for her again – she'll find her… won't you Cassie?

CASSIE. Yeah I'll… I've just got to… Tin – give your sister a big hug for me, alright. And don't let go till I'm back.

Sound out. KIT tries to shake off the memory and addresses the audience.

KIT. Er… now we're going to do a bit of the play that's a bit sad and I believe in you and I know you can be brave, but just in case I'm going to give this person my hat that's a frog.

She gives the hat to an audience member and encourages them to wear it.

Don't worry I haven't got nits…

The audience member puts it on.

…any more. Are we ready? Action –

Scene Nine – Bowling – April 2023

Bowling sound. TIN and CASSIE are sitting down. KIT is practising her dance moves and can't hear them.

CASSIE. Wit-woo, what's his name?

TIN. Jake Hawkins. But what would I have to do, like? Hold his hand and do a dance with him like people in films?

CASSIE. Only if you wanted to. Anyway why's he asking you now, it's ages off?

TIN. What about Kit though? If I were holding hands and dancing with Jake who's gonna make sure she dun't get lonely or sad, or run off or come home with pockets full of Party Rings again?

CASSIE. Kit'll be alright... You gotta think about yourself sometimes. It's your last Christmas Disco at Greenwoods and if you want to go with this Jake Hawkins then that's what you do.

TIN. I'll have to think about it. Have you ever gone t'disco with anyone?

CASSIE. Er... no. No I just never /

KIT (*mid-dance move*). / What souvenirs do you reckon she's got us?

TIN. What?

KIT (*coming over*). Mum. From her holidays.

CASSIE. Kit... don't think about that for now eh, er... oh I forgot... how were your animal project day?

KIT. Good thanks; my hat kept falling off so I asked Chloe Lee to Pritt Stick it to my head at first break, and she said that were daft cos I'd have a Pritt Sticky head but she did it anyway and now I've got a Pritt Sticky head. Alice put it in the wash and I'm dead miffed.

TIN. Depends where she's been what souvenirs she brings you know. If it's Spain, she might get us them maracas, like them flamenco dancers off telly

KIT. Ahhh yeah yeah or if she's been to France she might get us some croissants

TIN. Don't be daft you can get them in Asda

KIT. No but proper French ones like bonjour /

CASSIE. / Look forget about souvenirs eh… eh Tin – did you get Mark and Alice to help you fill out that form to get your telescope from t'borough?

TIN. Yeah, I've just got to write one hundred words about why it'll help with learning and stuff and then Alice'll drop it int' social on her way /

KIT. / D'you think she'll be back soon Cassie, cos I don't want her to miss your birthday?

Silence. CASSIE *turns away, trying not to say anything.* TIN *notices this.*

TIN. Kit, maybe let's stop talking about her for a bit yeah, it makes Cassie sad

we can talk about her in our bedroom	KIT. I don't want to make Cassie sad,
CASSIE. Kit listen, it's…	I don't want to make Cassie sad…
Look, Kit /	

Jasmine's voice interrupts them from the other side of the bowling alley.

JASMINE. / Cassie! I knew you'd be here

CASSIE. Oh… hiya… Jaz look it's not the best /

JASMINE. / Come over I've got summat to tell you, come on Cassie!

CASSIE. Okay… girls I'll be two minutes alright sit still and have your slushies yeah?

CASSIE *goes over to Jasmine. Over the following,* KIT *spills her slushie and* TIN *has to clean it up, distracting her so* KIT *can go to* CASSIE.

JASMINE. So I were just on my phone just now right and I get this email and I'm like who's emailing me at like seven o'clock at night right and I look and it's from that summer school, the media production one right and Cass – I got in… I can't fucking believe it… Mum's round telling all the neighbours now

CASSIE. Jaz that's brilliant... fuck, yeah that's... I probably won't though, so /

JASMINE. / Oh come on... course you will and I bet you'll get the scholarship – and if you don't we'll get the money from somewhere, look when was the last time you checked your email? Come on, I'll look, what's your login? /

CASSIE. / Jaz I never applied... I never even finished the first form

JASMINE. What? Cassie what you on about /

CASSIE. / I know, it's fine you'll just go, you'll have a great time /

JASMINE. / No, no way Cass, it's not too late, fucking go home right now and finish it, then ring 'em in t'morning

CASSIE. Maybe... But... no, I can't leave the girls /

JASMINE. / What? They'll stay with Alice and... whatever he's called... they'll be fine...

CASSIE. No, look Jaz, people like me don't go to summer schools
They don't go anywhere...   JASMINE. What y'on about
Definitely not to bloody   people like you?
London cos they have people
who need them cos if I go, for
a whole month, who's going
to pick 'em up from school
eh?
A nanny? Cos it won't be   It's not your bloody job
Mark and Alice. And that's
another person they don't know, and they definitely won't
fucking need me any more /

JASMINE. / You're smart Cass! Your animation stuff's incredible you'll fucking walk in – look think about having that on your UCAS

KIT. Cassie...

JASMINE. Oh for fuck's sake

CASSIE. In a minute, Kit.
Jaz can we talk about this
later?

KIT. Cassie what can I do
to make you not be sad, I
don't want you to be sad

JASMINE. Fine, whatever, if you
wanna chuck this chance away
that's up to you – but I'm
going. You can do what the
fuck you like

Sorry Jasmine but Cassie
just needs to listen to me
right Cassie listen 'sall
gonna be brill right we'll
only be living at Mark and
Alice's for a few more days
or maybe even just one
more day cos Mum's just
gone on holidays and

CASSIE. Oh fuck off man that's
not fair

Oh my God she hasn't...
She hasn't Kit I can't keep... She's fucked off somewhere –
probably cos she were sick of me telling her to be better
when she didn't want to be. My fault. So just go and sit back
down. Please.

CASSIE *turns away.* KIT *looks around –* TIN *is still cleaning
up spilled slushie and hasn't heard what has happened.* KIT
runs away.

JASMINE. Cass...

CASSIE. Alright Jaz, I'll do it. I'll fill out the form. So maybe I
can come with you /

JASMINE. / No Cass – your sister's gone.

Music. CASSIE *runs to* TIN. *Panicked improvisation as*
CASSIE *pulls* TIN *through the bowling alley, looking for
their sister.* KIT *appears in the audience.*

KIT. I don't know for suresies why I ran away from't bowling

CASSIE. We ran so hard looking for her – neon bowling lights
burning into us like fire

KIT. So I couldn't really give people from t'social a proper
answer when they asked

CASSIE. Proper pegged it

KIT. I think my brain were so full of thoughts I couldn't think one sure one

TIN. 'Part from at school I'd never not been able to see her before – since she were born – not even out the corner of my eye

KIT. But I knew it were all my fault cos I told Mrs Phillips and that were why Social took us and because of that Cassie were sad… and the only way to fix that were to find Mum.

CASSIE. And I didn't want to ask a grown-up cos that'd be like me saying I can't do it; that they needed Mark and Alice – that I wasn't enough.

KIT. I didn't know where like – and if she had gone to France that'd be hard to get to cos I only had fifty pee and a bowling sticker

TIN. And I knew she only had fifty pee and a bowling sticker so she couldn't get bus or owt

CASSIE. And all I kept thinking was that I'm all they've got now. That this is my job now. To find her. And to save her.

Music out.

KIT. But wherever Mum were… I knew it were over the other side of the big road.

Beat. She runs through the audience into the road, and is hit by an oncoming car. Low and threatening sound.

TIN. By the time we got there, a lady with a Labrador had wrapped her in her coat and were calling an ambulance, and an old bloke with a cap on were keeping the traffic stopped with his walking stick

CASSIE. She looked so small lying on the ground…

TIN. The driver had seen her and slammed brakes on so she hadn't been hit full-on like – just hard enough to knock her over

CASSIE. Crying and shaking…

TIN. And to break her leg… in two different places.

CASSIE. She ran away because she wanted to make her family fixed when she knew it were broken. I couldn't leave – not for London, not for anywhere.

TIN. Cassie asked her before we got in the ambulance if there was owt that'd make her stop feeling scared, and she said her frog hat, so I called Mark and Alice on the ambulance phone and they came with it dead fast

CASSIE. I'd been selfish. Just like Mum was, and so I'd hurt them, just like Mum did. I needed to be better... and summat needed to change – to keep them safe. To fix my family.

Scene Ten – The Hospital

Music. Sat on hospital chairs, TIN *is asleep on* CASSIE.

KIT*'s plaster is drying. She is half-asleep. She is wearing her frog hat wonkily, and* CASSIE *tries to straighten it.*

CASSIE (*smiling*). Kit it's still covered in Pritt Stick – let me rinse it in t'sink

KIT. But it's my hat that's a frog

CASSIE. I know... and frogs love the water so it'll be well into it, come on! (*Beat.*) Why'd you ask for it? In the ambulance. Why your hat?

KIT. Cos... when it's on my head... it's easier to like... think the answers when I do my homework. And to have ideas for fun games when we're playing out... Cos you got it for me...

BOTH. From the Oxfam shop

KIT. And it makes me remember that you love me, and how while Mum's on holidays you're all I've got... and how you want me to be the brightest star in the sky and stuff... And it makes me feel safe. (*Beat.*) And that's why I wear my hat that's a frog.

They are quiet for a moment. CASSIE puts her hand on the back of KIT's head to comfort her and feels how sticky the hat is again.

CASSIE. It's proper sticky though

Beat.

KIT. Yeah it's gross

CASSIE. Right, shall we do the next bit. Up we get

They help KIT stand up with her crutches.

Scene Eleven – Mark and Alice's – April 2023

The girls are coming in from school – KIT is on crutches. They talk to Mark and Alice by looking out.

MARK. Hiya girls /

KIT. / Why are there balloons in a Waitrose bag behind t'coat rack?

ALICE. Oh… you saw those…

MARK. Er… don't worry about them for now – did you have a good day?

TIN. Yeah, it were super-good thanks – we did a nature walk in t'park and I touched some frogspawn real gentle like and it felt like when Cassie used to make strawberry jelly

KIT. Yeah and I got Chloe Lee to sign my cast, look she drew a massive /

CASSIE. / Come on girls you've got homework, *(Preparing the girls to go upstairs.)* and my history coursework's due tomorrow so /

ALICE. / Er… we just quickly wanted to all get together in the living room

MARK. And we've got a special tea on – those oven chips you like, and chicken goujons /

KIT. Oooh bonjour /

ALICE. / Cos… we've got something to ask Tin and Kit. Something big.

MARK. We've had such a fantastic time getting to know you girls – all three of you – over the last four months; we really care about you and we love looking after you /

ALICE. / and we don't want it to stop… We don't want to stop looking after you.

MARK. And with Cassie starting to look at unis /

CASSIE. / I mean, I'm probably not going, cos /

MARK. / or whatever she wants to do… we wanted to ask you, Tin and Kit, if…

ALICE. Girls… we want to adopt you.

Silence.

CASSIE *(quietly)*. What? /

ALICE. / We know how hard it's been for you, and we know this doesn't just fix everything that's happened to you – but we want us to be a family…

CASSIE. Is this just cos of /
the crash?

MARK. / It'll not be the same as your family with your mum, we know that, and you can keep calling us just Mark and Alice for as long as you like but… we'll be together.

KIT. Till our mum comes back you mean?

Beat.

CASSIE. No Kit…

ALICE. Love… We don't know if /

MARK. / if she is…

TIN (*scared*). What do you mean… what do you mean of course
she is

CASSIE. You don't even know them, it's been four months /

ALICE. / Of course; if your mother came back, of course that'd
be different, but now /

CASSIE (*quietly*). / They don't need to be adopted.

MARK. We just want you to be a part of our family… /

CASSIE (*stronger*). / They don't need to be adopted because
I can look after them.

Silence.

ALICE. Cassandra… (*Correcting herself.*) Cassie… I don't
think you know what you're saying /

CASSIE. / You guys've been great, thank you, and it's been a
great break for us, but… I know what I need to do now.
I have since the crash. She got hurt cos I… lost my focus for
a minute… I forgot what were important. But that's gonna
change – I am gonna be one-hundred-percent focused on
them now, I am gonna try harder… push myself harder,
to be the best mu– best… Cassie… I can be for them. *I*
understand them. *I* love them. I know you don't believe I can
do it right but I will show you, I'll show the Social, I'll show
everyone… that I can care for them /

MARK. / You… need to think about your… future… Cassie…
having time to do the work for your A levels /

ALICE. / going to university… you can't take your sisters with
you can you?

CASSIE. Well then I won't go

TIN. Cassie…

CASSIE. Cos if I were there who'd pick them up when you
were at Pilates, eh? Would you send someone else to get
them if they were your own kids? It dun't matter how much

you spend at Waitrose, or how many clubs you sign them up for, or how many fancy fucking balloons you buy, they don't need a new family cos I am their family – they are not yours to adopt – you're not our parents… you are not part of our family. Do you understand? We don't need you. We don't need anyone.

Silence.

MARK. We don't need to be your parents to be your family Cassie. (*Beat.*) We care about you – we love you…

CASSIE (*under her breath as she leaves to sit behind the audience*). Fuck off

MARK. All of you.

Silence.

ALICE. Look we'll… take the balloons away, eh. Give you some time… however much time you need.

There is a horrible, awkward pause. The lights, including the house lights, come up, and KIT *puts away her crutches.* TIN *gets a mic, which she talks into, and gives to the audience to talk into.*

Transition – The Audience

TIN. Hiya everyone – we wanted to ask you summat right cos… we're not sure about lots of stuff, and it's getting a bit scary…

KIT. People think we're too little to know things but we're brave. I went to Chloe Lee's sleepover and we watched a 12A and I only cried like three times… that's a win

TIN (*introducing an audience member*). This is _____. We met _____ at the beginning and they were dead nice – _____ do you think we should get adopted by Mark and Alice, or go back to living with Cassie?

She gives the mic to the audience member who has been asked if they're okay with this during the pre-set. If the audience member chooses Mark and Alice, TIN's next line should start with 'But' as she is disagreeing with them, if they choose Cassie it should start with 'Yeah cos' as she is agreeing with them.

The AUDIENCE MEMBER *answers.*

TIN. ['But' *or* 'Yeah cos'] we don't know for sure when mum's coming back – so they shouldn't adopt us... right? Cos if they did and then Mum came back they'd have to give us back to Mum and change our second names back again and it'd just be such a palaver... AND if they adopted us what'd we call Alice – Mum, or just Alice?

KIT. Yeah right, cos Alice is a dead-nice name, but /

CASSIE (*from behind the audience*). / You'd just call her Alice... She's not your mum... So she's just Alice.

An awkward moment as this hangs in the air.

KIT. Sorry.

TIN (*trying to shake the moment off*). Who's in your family ____?

The AUDIENCE MEMBER *answers.*

TIN. Yeah cos there's loads of different people that could be your family right? Jake Hawkins lives with his grandma and a really big cat

KIT. Yeah and Chloe Lee lives with her dads who adopted her when she were a baby, and they make dead-nice ratatouille. (*A decision.*) Anyone could look after us if they were kind. Anyone who really loves us. That's what I think.

Music. CASSIE *returns to the stage as if entering the lawyer's office, and sits nervously with her sisters standing behind her.*

Scene Twelve – Lawyer's Office – May 2023

LAWYER. It's nice to meet you Cassie.

CASSIE. Nice to meet you Mr Clarke

LAWYER. Call me Dan.

TIN. They'd asked on the phone if Cassie were short for anything. She said it weren't.

LAWYER. There's lots of cases like yours, so don't worry; you're not on your own.

CASSIE. It felt kinda like everything in the room were made for grown-ups – chair where my feet didn't quite touch the floor, and fancy words I didn't understand like that night at the Social. But he had a kind face.

LAWYER. Just so we're clear – you're asking the court to put Tina and Kitten in your care. You can apply for a special guardianship order when you're eighteen, but until then we're proposing a child arrangement order, bolstered by a supervision order in favour of the local authority.

KIT. And she had that feeling you get when you've started summat so massive it could get out of control real quick… like pressing blast-off on a rocket

CASSIE. And he told me I'd definitely get legal aid cos we're in care, which is where they pay for some of it at least, so that were good

KIT. There were nothing left of Mum's dole money Cassie'd kept in her pencil case.

LAWYER. The professional witnesses will be your social worker, an independent social worker and a child and adolescent psychologist. After watching you with your sisters they'll create a Contract of Expectations, which will review and feedback to you about your performance as a carer, and what areas they expect you to improve in. After another period of observation allowing you to address these areas, the ISW will do a report for a viability assessment and advise if they think you'll be a suitable placement option... But the judge is the decision-maker.

The rumble of a rocket.

TIN. And every word he said the rocket flew higher and faster into space.

KIT. There were no stopping it now.

CASSIE. I just... I want better for them than what I had.

LAWYER. I know.

CASSIE. Dan... If they judge against me and Mark and Alice adopt them – could they cut our contact?

LAWYER. Well... yes, but I'm sure from what you've told me...

CASSIE. But they could?

TIN. On a mission to find the trinary star system

LAWYER. If Mark and Alice were to request it, and it is determined to be in the girls' best interests... any further contact between you and your sisters could be prohibited until their eighteenth birthdays.

BOTH. ...and to keep it safe.

Transition – A Play Within a Play

Music out. A beat. Lights change. The sisters start to set up for the puppet show. There is an sense that keeping going with the play is becoming increasingly difficult.

TIN. Erm... now we're going to do what's called a play-within-a-play... We did it in drama club, it's like in *A Midsummer Night's Dream*, when /

CASSIE. / Tin, are you sure – we can just skip this bit if you want – they won't mind

TIN. Oh… er /

KIT. / In a world full of liars, it's important that everyone has all the facts, so that the truth can be a force for good. (*Beat.*) They said that on *Power Rangers*.

CASSIE. Okay well… say if you want to stop yeah?

They act out the following with Mr Potato Head, Elephant and a sock puppet on a makeshift puppet stage.

Scene Thirteen – Bowling, December 2022

CASSIE. Right, I've given Mum the money to get the slushie, so just sit tight and – Kit what you doing?

TIN. Kit found this bowling ball, and she said it were green like her frog hat, and I found this dead-nice blue one that looks like t'night sky – so I thought we could scratch our names on the bottom with my compass so we could always find them /

CASSIE. / You can't… well alright you're doing it now but just make sure no one sees!

TIN. Have we not got money for just one game Cassie?

KIT. And can we get blue-flavour slushie please?

CASSIE. Tin you know we're only here to watch the other people bowl and keep warm cos the… radiator's broken again… yeah? And Kit you'll get whatever slushie Mum gets, now just both sit down till she gets back yeah?

KIT (*leaning forward to look*). I can't see Mum in t'slushie queue. Are you sure she's getting them Cassie?

CASSIE. Maybe she's just gone t'loo – do you want me to go check?

KIT. Yes please.

CASSIE. Okay well sit still and hold Tin's hand; I'll be back in a minute.

TIN holds up a clock and puts the hand forward twenty minutes.

TIN. You were gone a long time...

KIT. Were she there?

CASSIE. Er... yeah. Yeah she were, she's just going to queue now...

The girls look and can't see her.

Er... at the other counter, by the Wimpy. I'll go and help her. Just sit tight yeah...

TIN holds up a clock and puts the hand forward forty-minutes. KIT cries. CASSIE abandons the puppets to comfort her. TIN is torn between the puppets and comforting her sister, but she has to continue.

TIN. Kit it's alright – there's just a long line at t'slushie counter I bet there is. Maybe machine's broken again and she's just waiting for them to fix it. Cassie's just on the phone – she'll find her won't you Cassie?

CASSIE. Yeah I'll... I've just got to... Tin – give your sister a big hug for me alright. And don't let go till I'm back.

The play is over. Silence apart from KIT crying.

(*Taking off the sock puppet.*) Tin can you put this away please?

TIN awkwardly puts everything back where it was.

KIT (*crying*). I don't want to do it anymore...

CASSIE. I know... It's okay, it's okay... Do you want to stand with me while we do the next bit?

CASSIE takes KIT's hand before picking up a microphone.

KIT stands with her head buried in CASSIE's hair.

Transition – Letter, September 2023

CASSIE. Hi Mum – girls went back to school today. Alice took Pilates off so we all could go to the park after we picked them up. They were so happy to see her... Kit came flying at her, told her all about how she'd got Angel Gabriel in t'nativity... Dani Hoskins and her sister walked past us at swings – whispering how we were posh twats now with our fancy new mum. They used to whisper about how slaggy it were the three of us had different dads and our mum didn't know who they were and now... Alice put her hand on my arm and told me to just pretend I didn't hear 'em. She's being dead nice... even though the independent social worker keeps coming round to watch me with the girls. The Social were supposed to give me this... contract thing... telling me stuff they want me to improve on as a carer so I could be better and show the judge I'm ready for this but they've not... even though the lawyer bloke keeps on asking them. Sometimes I reckon they'd decided what they thought before they met me... And tomorrow's the psychologist assessment. Tin's so nervous about it she keeps waking up in the night. So Alice said we should go to the café bit and get ice creams for a treat.

KIT. Ice cream?

CASSIE. Yeah, do you wanna get one?

KIT. Ice cream!!

> KIT *runs off.*

CASSIE. And me and Tin just had Mini Milks – me cos they were cheapest and Tin cos someone'd told her there were a joke on the stick when you finished it. But Kit...

> KIT *re-enters with a huge Mr Whippy ice cream with a Flake, sauce and sprinkles, which she eats over the following. It is the best thing she has ever eaten in her life.*

Before I could stop her she pointed at the biggest one – like, a ninety-nine with all the stuff on – raspberry sauce, a flake, sprinkles, the lot; and Alice didn't say a word, just smiled and passed the man a twenty-quid note. (*Laughs at the memory.*) And I know to most kids that'd be just any Thursday after school but to her... To be able to have summat that she really wanted just like her friends can... to sit on the grass with this massive ice cream and feel the melting bit dripping off her chin and for her to be told she deserves something and feel like she matters and to have someone who can make her feel like that every day... I will love her every minute of every day for the rest of her life – and I can make her packed lunches and make sure she's got her homework diary in her school bag... but I can't get her a new party dress for the end-of-year disco... I can't buy birthday presents for her friends when she gets invited to parties, I can't help her with her uni fees when she's older, I can't even buy her a fucking ice cream... (*These realisations have really upset her.*) I can't give her what they can... So maybe we really do need them. Maybe I'm just not enough. And if you're not coming back – maybe they should be their mum and dad.

KIT *has finished, and her face and hands are covered in ice cream and sauce.*

(*To* KIT.) You are covered. Come here.

KIT *goes to* CASSIE *and presents her face, whilst* CASSIE *cleans her with wet wipes.*

Scene Fourteen – Mark and Alice's – November 2023

Lights change. TIN *is reading* Great Expectations.

She finds a picture in between the pages of the book.

TIN. Cassie?

CASSIE (*still cleaning* KIT). Yeah hold on a minute mate.

TIN. Cassie look what I've found in *Great Expectations* – it's a baby, look!

She shows CASSIE. *It is a scan of a baby.* KIT *looks over as she lies down, tired.*

Were it Mark and Alice's do you think? Did it... did it never get born?

Beat.

CASSIE. No... I don't think it did

KIT. Is that why they want to adopt us?

CASSIE. Yeah maybe...

TIN. Why do they not think Mum's coming back? Do they know a secret?

CASSIE. They don't know any secret don't worry – they don't know whether she's coming back or not they just – grownups just make guesses sometimes... and then decide them guesses are true.

TIN. Never assume...

KIT. Cos it makes an ass out of you and me... dead good that because I get to say 'ass'...

CASSIE. Look come here

Pulling them to her. Beat. She steels herself.

Listen... if Mum... if she has to stay away... for a long time... or maybe forever, then

TIN. There is a secret... There is a secret and you know it too!

CASSIE. No Tin there isn't, I'm just saying, if that was what happened, *if*, then... you'd want me to be the one to look after you... right?

KIT. Do you not want her to come back?

CASSIE. Kit of course I /

KIT. / It's like you don't, you know – it's like you don't want us to have Mark and Alice /

TIN. / And you don't want us to have Mum either /

CASSIE. / No Tin /

TIN. / She is our mum! And she holds our hands in the dark even when she is not there /

KIT. / She picks us up from school and gets us treats on the way home /

TIN. / She does our homework with us and helps us spell things right /

KIT. / she loves us and stands by us in the night and keeps us safe from the monsters

CASSIE (*an explosion that has been building for the whole of her sisters' lives*). She doesn't!

A horrible silence.

She doesn't... She has never done those things, those are the things that I do! That mum that you are talking about, that is not our mum – that is the mum you have read about in your stories, in your daydreams and in your fucking library books... Our mum missed your injections when you was a baby cos she were sleeping off the night before

so you got measles! Our	TIN. she must have been
mum left your pram in the	tired...
park and we had to beg a	
judge to give you back	KIT. she were poorly!

...and our mum spent the money she should've spent on you on fucking... (*Cries.*) And you've forgotten all that... haven't you? You've forgotten some of it and just never noticed the rest because you're young and little and happy and I understand why, but when you're bigger and taller and older you will see then and you will know and you'll realise that she has broken you inside... (*Takes a breath. A decision.*) I will not let anyone break you any more... (*Slowly.*) I am going to take care of you. I will be your mum and your dad and your sister. Just. Me.

Urgent driving music. TIN *and* KIT *exit.*

CASSIE *is running to the bowling alley. She picks up the mic and speaks into it.*

Dear Mum. If you're out there somewhere please, please
come home. The Social are hardly talking to me any more –
I just know unless you come back they're gonna take the
girls away. I'll forgive you... for everything Mum – for
letting Martin lock me out in the snow, for calling me a slag
and saying you wish you'd never had me... for giving me
a black eye... I'll forgive you... You won't even have to do
anything – you won't have to be our mum, you won't even
have to see us if you don't want to just please. Please. Come.
Home.

Scene Fifteen – Bowling

Music out. CASSIE *arrives at the bowling alley, dropping the
microphone. Exhausted and desperate, she puts the letter she
has written in the secret spot.*

*The musician puts on their cap to be the bowling attendant and,
seeing this, comes out from behind their instruments for the first
time.*

BOWLING ATTENDANT. Hiya – are you... is your name
Cassie by any chance?

CASSIE. Yeah? What do you want?

BOWLING ATTENDANT. I work here and er... I think I've got
some things that belong to you? We kept finding these...

*They hand her the letters the sisters have left at the bowling
for their mum.*

...under the rack by the spare balls. We read a couple and
they seemed pretty important so we thought we'd better not
chuck 'em. Then Rhona from t'popcorn counter saw you
leave one the other day, but you ran off before she could
catch you so when you came in just now I thought...

CASSIE. Yeah. (*Beat.*) Yeah of course...

BOWLING ATTENDANT. Can I do anything to help you? Can I call someone?

CASSIE. No... Thank you. I've just got to do this myself. Just me.

Scene Sixteen – School – December 2023

Music – 'O Come, O Come, Emmanuel'. CASSIE *puts on a blazer.* KIT *steps nervously out onto the stage for the nativity, and* TIN *sings.*

TIN *(sings)*. O come, O come, Emmanuel,
and ransom captive Israel

That mourns in lonely exile here,
until the Son of God appear

Rejoice! Rejoice! Emmanuel

shall come to thee,
O Israel.

KIT. And so it were that while they were there, the days were accomplished that she should be delivered. And she gave birth to her firstborn. She wrapped Him in swaddling cloths and laid Him in a manger, because there were no room for them in the inn. And suddenly there were with the angel a multitude of the heavenly host praising God, and saying, Glory to God in the highest, and on earth peace, goodwill toward men.

KIT *bows, then takes* TIN*'s hand and they run off.*

Scene Seventeen – The Court – 12th December 2023

CASSIE *gives an audience member a microphone and the court verdict.*

CASSIE. Could you read this please?

AUDIENCE MEMBER. In these care proceedings the options for the care of a group of two siblings, B aged eleven years and C aged eight years, are either care by their seventeen-year-old sister A, or placement for adoption. While A is completely committed to caring for her sisters, and can meet their basic care needs, she does not have the emotional attunement to fully understand the impact on her or on B and C of their neglected upbringings. They all say that B and C, who have insecure attachments, need reparative and attuned parenting by a carer who is able to anticipate their emotional needs – to be able to read them, as B and C's social worker said, or stay one step ahead as the psychologist put it. Impressed though everybody is by A, the unanimous view of the professionals is that she cannot meet those needs.

Quietly thanking the audience member, CASSIE *takes the verdict and microphone back. The* MUSICIAN *gently oohs an a capella reprise of 'O Come, O Come, Emmanuel'.* CASSIE *looks up to three light bulbs far above the set, hanging closely together with one slightly further away. The scene slowly dissolves around her and changes to the night of the disco.*

Scene Eighteen – Mark and Alice's

CASSIE. Are you nearly ready? Alice's heating up the car!

TIN. Ready!

CASSIE turns round and TIN *runs in in a blue dress covered in silver stars.* KIT *enters, unimpressed. Her dress is a dinosaur print and her hair is a mess.* CASSIE *is very . moved.*

CASSIE. You look... beautiful. Dead grown up. Come here Kit let me sort out that rat's nest.

KIT. Oi! Don't be a hater!

She reluctantly goes over and CASSIE *sorts her hair.*

CASSIE. How you feeling about Jake Hawkins then?

TIN. Proper psyched, thanks. He says he's getting me a corsage

KIT. Ooh bonjour

TIN. And I said what's that and he said he weren't sure he'd just heard about it on t'telly but Kit says if it's food she'll eat it /

KIT. / I will /

TIN. / so it's all good!

CASSIE. Fancy... And Kit you're gonna have to be good when your sister's off dancing – and leave some Party Rings for the others!

KIT. I'm not making any promises

CASSIE finishes KIT's hair and turns her round to look at her.

CASSIE. That's better.

KIT *goes over to where* TIN *is and looks at herself in the mirror.*

KIT (*Beat*). I'm gorgeous! When did that happen?

The two sisters giggle and pose together in the mirror. CASSIE *looks at them.*

CASSIE. Eh...

This is difficult for her, but she knows it's what the girls need to hear.

Mum'd be dead proud.

KIT. Yeah?

CASSIE. Yeah… promise.

TIN. Me and Kit were talking and… it's horrible sad that Mum's gone away, and we know that it might be a long time before she comes back but… being with Mark and Alice we think… we think it's not better and it's not worse, it's just… different… in't it? It's just a new bit of our story.

KIT. And we just need to keep… washing our hands, and breathing, and loving each other.

CASSIE. Yeah. We will. (*Breathes out.*) Right go on, get your coats, Alice's waiting.

TIN *and* KIT *go to the door.*

TIN. Cassie… It's okay that you're not going to be our mum y'know.

KIT. Cos you're our big sister.

TIN. And we love you more than all the stars there are.

Music. They dance, with improvised dialogue throughout. After a while TIN *and* KIT *wave goodbye and leave, and* CASSIE *is left alone. We transform back to the courtroom, as she steps up to make her case. The music continues under the following.*

Scene Nineteen – The Court – 10th December 2023

CASSIE. Erm… good afternoon everyone. Sorry, I'm not used to standing up in front of grown-ups like this… I am here today to talk about my sisters. On the eighteenth of December last year our mum took us to the Tempton Road Megabowl, went to get a slushie and never came back. She'd disappeared before, and I'd always just rung up one of her mates or the pub up the road and got her back before the girls noticed. But this time were different. So until the Social came I were looking after them just me. And it were really hard. It were hard before she left and it were hard after but... that weren't cos I'm seventeen... That were because it is hard caring for people – for anyone. Anyone can do anything... be anything... I think. I know that now. So open your mind for just a second – see a family that ain't just two adults and some kids, see me... me and them... I am one year away from being what you all call an adult, right, but if I wait till then for this they'll have two other people to have for forever and it'll be too late for me.

She looks up at the faces in the courtroom.

I can see you don't believe I can do this... Look, I have done everything I can to prove myself to all of you... The Social never sent that contract telling me what they wanted me to do better – even though Dan asked and asked – so for them to stand up here and say they don't believe in me is... How am I supposed to be better when they won't tell me what they think better is? (*Breaking.*) I love my sisters... I LOVE THEM with every tiny part of me and I swear to you, I am promising you, I'm... (*Looking around the room at their disbelieving faces.*) this is... I'm sorry for wasting your time.

Music out. Silence. She leaves the light and breaks for a moment.

She makes a decision and comes back to the light.

You know what right... my sister Tin has just turned eleven, but she knows more about science and space than anyone my age and probably anyone your age too... One night, when our little sister had just been born, she couldn't sleep, so we went out for a walk with her strapped to me, just as the night sky were coming out and the light were fading. And halfway round Tin looked up, and she stopped still on the pavement and couldn't stop looking. And then she said... with more joy in her voice than I'd ever heard in anyone's... 'Look – it's you and me and Kitten!' And I looked up at what she was; and it were three stars. Moving together in the sky. And they were dead bright even though it weren't properly night-time yet. And when we got home we looked it up in her space book and we found out those three stars go everywhere together – and two of the stars need the other one – the 'little-bit-further-away star' she calls it – cos it cares for the other two... and keeps them safe in the massive galaxy... Keeps them safe in the darkness. And she pointed at that third star in the book and said 'Cassie that one's you.'

Music begins to build up again.

So even if you don't think I can do this it doesn't matter. Because she does. They both do. And I will love them – wherever I am – I will love them more than all the stars there are. Thank you.

Scene Twenty – Epilogue

TIN *and* KIT *enter and stand either side of* CASSIE.

TIN. And she finished her UCAS form and she sent it off

KIT. And she knew that it were time for the next part of her story

TIN. And the night before she left she took us out into Mark and Alice's back garden and we looked up at the sky.

CASSIE *holds her sisters' hands and they look at the stars.*

KIT. And the starlight lit us up like magic and she held on to us tight, so just for that moment we wouldn't fly away

CASSIE. Just Cassie and the lights.

A moment of music and improvisation as the sisters watch the stars together. Then CASSIE *takes the two hands she was holding and puts them together, before walking towards a bright light.*

TIN. And we said 'We'll be here under the stars with you forever. Won't we Cassie? Won't we Cassie?'

Music out.

Almost gone, CASSIE *looks back at her sisters.*

BOTH. Won't we?

Lights out.

The End.

Acknowledgements

Thanks to Caroline for giving our house over to suitcases,
Meaghan and Oli, without whom none of this would have been
possible, Xinyi Shen, Sam Brain & Zoe Weldon, Mia Campbell,
Arts Council England, Become Charity, Participation People,
Andrew and Chantal Mackley, Lizzie Williams, Saul Valiunas,
Sam Rayner, Grahame Edwards, Ruth Redman, Phoebe Coco,
Teresa Origone, Alexandra Golebiowski and family, but most
of all, every child and young person I spoke to when writing the
play. Without your openness, honesty and generosity it wouldn't
exist.

A.H.

A Nick Hern Book

Cassie and the Lights first published in Great Britain as a paperback original in 2024 by Nick Hern Books Limited, The Glasshouse, 49a Goldhawk Road, London W12 8QP, in association with Patch of Blue and 3 hearts canvas, Southwark Playhouse and Verse Unbound

Cover artwork by Casey Jay Andrews

Designed and typeset by Nick Hern Books, London
Printed in Great Britain by Mimeo Ltd, Huntingdon, Cambridgeshire PE29 6XX

A CIP catalogue record for this book is available from the British Library

ISBN 978 1 83904 333 8

www.nickhernbooks.co.uk/environmental-policy